Series Editor: Catherine Bowness

The
Faith in
Action
Series

A Modern Martyr

··

The Story of Oscar Romero

Liam Gearon

Illustrated by Brian Platt

RMEP

RELIGIOUS AND MORAL EDUCATION PRESS

A MODERN MARTYR

···

The Story of Oscar Romero

The year is 1980. The place is a small country in Central America called El Salvador. In 1980, it is a country troubled by civil unrest, rioting and violence. In the capital city of San Salvador, this particular Sunday seems little different from any other Sunday. Imagine yourself there.

This Sunday evening the Archbishop of San Salvador, a leader of the Roman Catholic Church, is holding a special service: an anniversary Mass to remember and pray for the deceased mother of Jorge Pinto, a friend of the Archbishop. Jorge Pinto owns a weekly newspaper, *El Independiente,* whose offices have been bombed only weeks before the Mass. Around the city, newspapers have advertised the fact that the Archbishop will be saying the Mass. There is nothing unusual about this. Within the Roman Catholic Church it is usual to announce the time of a service of remembrance so that local people can join the family and friends in prayer for the soul of the deceased person. However, some of the Archbishop's friends are worried about the publicity surrounding this event. The Archbishop has made enemies.

This particular Mass is being held in the chapel of a San Salvadorian hospital. Much of the work of this hospital is in treating cancer. As it happens, it is a hospital for which the Archbishop has helped to raise much-needed funds. During the Mass, the well-known Psalm 23 is read: 'The Lord is my shepherd ... Though I walk through the valley of the shadow of death, I fear no evil ....'

While the Mass is going on a number of men approach the chapel. They are middle aged, wearing ordinary civilian clothes. There is nothing to mark them out from the rest of the congregation. They could be local Catholics arriving late for the service, but they remain outside. Some witnesses later say these are police in plain clothes.

The Archbishop reaches the end of his sermon. He has talked about the simple and selfless life of the mother of his friend. He speaks about the part of the Mass where bread and wine are blessed, the point when Christians remember the last supper of Jesus. It is also the time when Christians recall the death of Jesus on the cross: 'May we give our body and blood to suffering and to pain – like Christ, not for self, but to teach justice and peace to our people. So let us join together intimately in faith and hope at this moment of prayer ...'

Suddenly a loud explosion is heard. Shots have been fired. The Archbishop, standing at the altar, falls backwards, wounded in the chest. In the mall hospital chapel, there is shock and confusion. Even in a ountry accustomed to violence, people in the congregation do ot know what to do. A newspaper photographer begins to take ictures. A nun is in tears near the fallen body of the rchbishop.

No one inside the chapel has a clear idea of what has just appened. An assassin's bullet had been shot through the open oor of the chapel. Outside, a red Volkswagen car is waiting and he assassin escapes. So it is reported: the facts of the case are ever made clear in a court of law.

The Archbishop is transferred to a specialist hospital, but is ead on arrival. Doctors at the emergency unit say that the 2-year-old man brought to them fatally wounded was killed by single .22 calibre bullet straight into the heart. The name of he assassinated Archbishop is Oscar Romero.

What Do You Think?

Important: in answering 'What Do You Think?' questions in this book, it is important that you not only state your opinion but also give as many reasons as possible for your opinion.

1. Why do you think anyone would want to kill an archbishop?

2. If you had been a member of the congregation, kneeling in prayer, in the hospital chapel, what would have been your first reaction when the shots rang out?

3. A newspaper editor might think more people would buy their paper if it reported the shooting of an archbishop in a church as an 'extra shocking' event. What headline might be on the front of the paper? Should news be reported in order to shock readers or to dramatize tragic events?

The World Reacts

There was shock and revulsion throughout the world following the killing of the Archbishop. What made matters worse was that the days after the assassination were marked with more violence in El Salvador. Pictures and stories of the violent events in the capital and throughout the country were shown on television and reported in newspapers around the globe.

By eerie coincidence the news of Romero's assassination reached England just as a new Archbishop of Canterbury, Robert Runcie, was about to attend his enthronement (appointment ceremony) at Canterbury Cathedral. One English newspaper reported that it was:

> ' ... strange that news of the killing of Archbishop Oscar Romero in El Salvador broke on the day of the enthronement of Robert Runcie. It's many centuries since the assassination of an Archbishop of Canterbury, but priests in Latin America live on the frontiers of violence.'

At the service of enthronement for the new Archbishop of Canterbury, prayers were said for Archbishop Romero. The congregation in Canterbury contained representatives from many of the world's Christian communities and in his sermon Robert Runcie asked all to remember the murder of Oscar Romero. He said that being a Christian, and being a Christian leader, meant that sometimes a person had to make great sacrifices. The death of Archbishop Romero was a reminder that this could mean being called to make the greatest sacrifice of all: to give up one's own life.

As a Christian, Romero felt that to live out this ideal of sacrifice an archbishop had to get involved in the life of the people. The politics of El Salvador at the time were very complicated, but many say that the Archbishop died for a very simple reason. They believe that Oscar Romero was killed because he was a spokesperson for the people, especially the poor, against a small but rich and powerful group of political rulers.

But how did Oscar Romero come to be such an important symbol of the Christian faith in modern times? How did Oscar Romero become 'a modern martyr'?

What Do You Think?

1. Is making a personal sacrifice (giving something up) for others an idea that people can understand today? If yes, why? If no, why not?

2. In the Middle Ages, Archbishop Thomas Becket was murdered in Canterbury Cathedral. He had told the King that he was behaving badly and not ruling the people properly. Oscar Romero may have died because he had criticized the government of El Salvador. Should priests be prepared to speak out when they believe that a nation's leaders are acting badly? Give reasons for your answer.

3. Martyrdom means sacrificing one's own life for something that one believes in. Is this something that religious people should still be ready to do or is this just a waste of life? Give reasons for your answer.

Oscar's Childhood

Oscar Romero was born on 15 August 1917 in Ciudad Barrios, in an isolated region within El Salvador. El Salvador is a small country: its total land area is only 21 393 square kilometres (8260 square miles). Located in Central America, El Salvador has a coastal border along the Pacific Ocean in the south. To the north and west is the country of Guatemala, while to the north and east is Honduras. Spanish is the official language of the people but, probably because of the closeness to the United States, English is also widely spoken.

El Salvador is a land of great physical beauty, with its range of landscapes from mountains to Pacific coastline. Ciudad Barrios is in the eastern part of the country, a small and remote village in the mountains.

It was a tough place in which to grow up. Oscar's parents were not well off. In 1903 Oscar's father Santos was sent to Ciudad Barrios from the nearby town where he had grown up, twenty kilometres away. The Government had put him in charge of the local telegram office, where he also acted as postmaster for the region. But the post office, where people would come to send their mail and telegrams, was actually part of the Romero home! It was a busy household with many children about. Oscar was the second oldest in the family, with an elder brother called Gustavo. Then there were five other children: Zaida, Romulo, Mamerto, Arnoldo and Gaspar. A sister, Aminta, died soon after birth.

Along with the other children, Oscar helped to supplement the family income from an early age. Whenever he could he assisted with the deliveries of mail and other messages. In a remote region like Ciudad Barrios the poor peasants living there depended greatly upon the mail. It was their main source of communication with the outside world, since travel was difficult in this harsh terrain.

The Romero family were lucky enough to have a few hectares of farmland too, just outside the village. The land, about eight hectares, had been inherited by Oscar's mother, Guadalupe de Jesus. They grew small amounts of coffee and grazed a few cows, which the children, including Oscar, learned how to milk.

Many people struggled, though, to make a living or even survive in Ciudad Barrios. There were families to feed

and work was scarce. Some felt they would rather struggle than move from their mountain home. Others, however, were forced by the harsh conditions to leave in order to find work.

There were not many opportunities for schooling either. When he was old enough Oscar went to the local school but it catered for only the first three grades, for pupils up to about the age of ten or eleven. Oscar's family had to arrange for a personal teacher for him when local schooling finished. Her name was Anita Iglesias and she taught him many subjects, but it was not cheap to pay for a personal teacher.

Oscar's father had taught him how to play a bamboo flute and he continued to like music with his new teacher. But when Oscar was about twelve, his father wanted him to work and not carry on any further with his studies. So he arranged for Oscar to be apprenticed to a local carpenter. Many villagers remember Oscar at that time as being a serious boy who would take the opportunity to pray in one of the two local churches after a hard day's work.

In 1930, when Oscar was thirteen, a priest returning from studies in Rome visited the village to say Mass. Oscar was already interested in religion and this Mass must have made a strong impression on him. He began to talk with people then about becoming a priest and joining a seminary to train. Even though he was just thirteen that is what he did.

Although they were poor, the people of Ciudad Barrios were deeply religious. They were almost without exception Roman Catholic Christians, as were most of the people of El Salvador. Here, the priest was an important and highly respected person. So, although Santos Romero did not want Oscar to go to the seminary he would have been proud of his son's achievements. Oscar would be one of the few local people with a proper education.

In some ways the priest was at the centre of community life. Sunday was an important day in the week for the Catholic community. It was a day when the priest, very much a man who lived a simple life amongst the people, would preach and celebrate Mass, which was always well attended. The priest would know well those at Sunday Mass. They were the same people with whom he would share important family occasions.

The priest would be present at all the religious ceremonies marking significant times in the villagers' lives. He would be at the baptisms of the infants and at the first Communions of the children.

The priest would be there at the weddings of couples who had chosen to marry and stay in Ciudad Barrios. It was the priest who would be there to comfort the sick and the dying. Amidst the poverty, then, the life of the community was centred around the life of the Church. To many, the Church was a sign, a presence of hope in a difficult life.

Oscar was an ordinary enough boy growing up in his home village. He enjoyed life. He played with his many friends. Often, though, he would pause for serious thought. Even as a young boy he reflected much upon the difficult lives of the people in Ciudad Barrios, especially their struggle for the basic necessities of life such as food and clothing. He saw how their faith was what kept the people going.

Oscar also had a strong religious faith. His belief in God gave him a sort of inner strength, and his friends and family all recognized this. He appeared at times to be able to rise above the difficult life which he lived. He almost seemed to smile at personal difficulty. The young Oscar knew that in the grand scheme of things, life held great meaning, that any suffering on earth was temporary. Still, he felt a huge commitment and responsibility to help people in whatever way he could. As a Catholic he felt that the best way he could help people would be to serve God as a priest.

What Do You Think?

1. Imagine that you are young Oscar and you are talking to your father about leaving home to study and become a priest. He does not really want you to leave. Suggest three things you would say to your father and three things he might say in reply.

2. The priest was at the centre of community life in Oscar's village. Think about your own community and describe it in a couple of sentences. What sorts of things does your community believe to be important? What would you expect a person at the centre of your community to do?

3. How are religious groups and their leaders involved in the daily lives of ordinary people in towns and villages throughout Britain?

4. Make a list of five words which could describe Oscar's childhood, e.g. 'happy', 'difficult'. Are your words mostly positive or mostly negative?

5. Oscar had to work hard as a child to help his family. What advantages or disadvantages are there for young people who are expected to work in order to help their family have a reasonable lifestyle?

Training to be a Priest

Oscar went to the nearest seminary, in a town called San Miguel. This was seven hours away on horseback, so he was able to get home only at holiday time. His studies went well and his family supported him as best they could. There is a story that he would send his washing home on a Friday with a local merchant and family friend who travelled the road from San Miguel to Ciudad Barrios. A mule would carry the laundry home and on Monday the merchant would bring it back cleaned!

Oscar showed so much promise that he was sent to a larger seminary in the capital, San Salvador. Again he was very successful in his studies. Later he had to leave South America and go to Europe to study in Rome itself, the ancient centre of the Catholic Church. But although training to be a priest meant leaving Ciudad Barrios, Oscar never forgot the poverty of the mountain village where he grew up. Nor did he forget the reason why he had decided to become a priest. He always remembered his personal mission to help make the lives of ordinary people better.

Oscar's studies in Rome, though, were a struggle. He had little money because his family were not at all wealthy and he had to spend several years away from family and friends in his home country. Despite this, he was a successful student.

In Rome during part of the Second World War, Oscar witnessed the devastation of war and a Europe torn apart by the struggle against evil in the world. This and his personal experience of poverty in his home village taught him many lessons about human suffering. When he returned to El Salvador in 1943, he was even more sensitive to the needs of ordinary people than he had been when he left home to train. As a new priest, he soon built up a reputation for working very hard for the people.

What Do You Think?

1. How do you think Oscar felt as he was leaving home and setting off for San Miguel to study?

Romero the Priest

When Romero was a young priest in the 1950s and 1960s, South America was a continent where many people were living in poverty, and this was no less true of El Salvador. Throughout the country many people were undernourished and without work, or in jobs that paid very little. Harsh governments, often headed by dictators, used the military to keep the majority of the people poor and the minority rich.

It was this sort of world that Romero encountered as a young priest. Very early on in his life as a priest, he was given responsibility for a parish in the mountains, a place quite similar to Ciudad Barrios, called Anamoros.

It was a difficult task to be a priest in a country with so many problems, but Romero rarely considered his own needs. He always sought to give comfort to others. Romero's sympathies were especially for the poor and he always looked for ways to lessen their burden. A modest and unassuming man, in his years as a priest Romero constantly prayed to God for guidance about how best to help the people.

Romero was a practical man, though, and knew that people's physical needs had to be met. Prayer had to be mixed with action. Romero would ensure that food was distributed to those who were really hungry. He would arrange shelter for those without homes. Often he would spend many days journeying amongst the people in difficult terrain. Sometimes he would just listen to people's problems, lending an ear to those who had no one else to tell their everyday stories of sorrow, loss or hardship.

A gentle man, with a winning smile, Romero also shared in the happy times of the people. Living a simple life, not seeking any great promotion, Romero was popular because the ordinary people, especially the poor, saw him as one of their own. After all, he came from an ordinary family.

The local bishop, however, soon felt he needed a man of Romero's intelligence to help him run the whole collection of parish districts that made up his diocese. So Romero, having settled into the life of Anamoros, found himself taking a job he was to do for twenty-three years: acting as personal assistant to the bishop in San Miguel, where he had first started his training. After his father died, Oscar's mother also settled in San Miguel.

Romero worked tirelessly for others in the diocese. A brilliant organizer and a great speaker, he became very well known in the region as he got involved in everything that was going on. He still travelled into the countryside to talk to people. In the city, he frequently visited prisoners in gaol. He worked with alcoholics, promoting the activities of Alcoholics Anonymous. He ensured that Caritas, a charity providing aid for the poor and hungry, also got involved in health education programmes. Romero became so well respected that he even took charge of the diocese in the absence of the bishop.

But Romero was a young priest at a time when both the world and the Church were changing greatly. Major developments in industry and technology led to great wealth in some countries. In contrast to South America, for example, ordinary people in North America (the United States and Canada), as well as in Europe, were beginning to have a much better standard of living. People's attitudes were changing too. They were becoming less likely to accept things as they were, less ready to accept authority without question.

In 1964, busy as ever in San Miguel, Romero heard and read about events in Europe, and about a conference being held in Rome. This conference was called the Second Vatican Council, or Vatican II. It seemed that the Roman Catholic Church was beginning to realize that the world was changing and that the Church must change too. However, such grand events seemed a long way from the everyday concerns of the poor Romero knew. He did take note, though, of one document that the bishops published. It was called *The Church in the Modern World* and its basic point was the need for fairness. Here is an extract:

> Great numbers of people are acutely conscious of being deprived of the world's goods through injustice and unfair distribution and are demanding their share. Developing nations are anxious to share in the political and economic benefits of modern civilization and to play their part freely in the world, but they are hampered by the economic dependence on the rapidly expanding richer nations and the ever widening gap between them. The hungry nations cry out to their affluent neighbours; women claim parity with men in fact as well as in rights; farmers and workers insist not just on the necessities of life but also on the opportunity to develop by their labour their personal talents ... Among nations there is a growing movement to set up a worldwide community.

In 1968 there was another big conference. This time the event was held in South America, in the city of Medellin in Colombia. The South American bishops realized that their continent had special problems that only the people of South America could really understand and help solve. This is how one writer summarized the situation:

> When the bishops of Latin America looked at their part of the world, they saw an area of 300 million people where most persons were Catholic but were poor and oppressed, where undernourishment and early death were the fate of millions, especially of children, and where modern social and economic development were worsening, rather than bettering, the lives of most inhabitants. The Church, they said, could no longer ignore such a situation and it had to raise its voice to proclaim the people's liberation. Injustice was not God's will.
>
> (James Brockman, *Romero: A Life,* Orbis Books, 1989)

Oscar Romero shared similar feelings about the poor and oppressed people of his own country, El Salvador. Later in his life, he would remember the message of these Church conferences, but helping the poor was what he had always done. It was one of the main reasons why he had become a priest.

What Do You Think?

1. Why do you think that many teachings of the major religions are concerned with issues of wealth and poverty?

2. Some areas of the world are very poor whilst others are rich. Suggest reasons for this. How would it be possible to have a more balanced distribution of wealth in the world?

3. What is injustice? What do you think is meant by the statement 'Injustice is not God's will'?

4. What do you think was meant by Vatican II's vision of a 'worldwide community'?

From Priest to Archbishop

Romero's caring attitude and genuine concern for ordinary people were recognized by the Church authorities. But he had also proved a reliable assistant to the bishop and thus, after twenty-three years in San Miguel, was appointed Secretary-General of the National Bishops' Conference. This meant moving to San Salvador. Three years later, in 1970, Romero was made auxiliary (assistant) bishop in San Salvador. In 1974, after over thirty years as a priest and at the direction of the Pope, Oscar Romero was given control of his own diocese, Santiago de Maria, which contained the parish of his birth, Ciudad Barrios.

Three years later, in 1977, aged 59, Oscar Romero was made Archbishop of San Salvador. He had shown himself to be a hard-working priest and bishop in some of the least hospitable parts of El Salvador. He had worked tirelessly for the people.

The image of El Salvador in the 1970s is of a troubled country and a troubled people. A rich and powerful elite, a ruling group of families, sometimes called an oligarchy, worked with the military to maintain their own luxurious lifestyles. The rich wanted to stay rich, and there was a great sense of injustice amongst the poor. Many people were terrified to speak out about their grievances for fear of the military, who helped to keep the Government in power and helped to keep the rich wealthy.

At the time when Oscar Romero was appointed Archbishop of San Salvador, the Church was divided on the important question: 'Should the Church get involved in politics?' Some priests, bishops and ordinary Christians thought that the Church should stick to religious matters and not speak out on things which were best left to the politicians. It was better for priests to lead people to the Kingdom of God than for them to start organizing society on earth.

However, other priests, bishops and lay people thought that the Church could not be separated from the world of politics. The people who thought the Church *should* get involved in politics were mostly the poor of the country and those siding with the poor. Such people wanted the Church to do more about the oppression by the Government and the military. They believed it only right that the wealth of El Salvador should be more evenly distributed – it was wrong that most of the wealth in the country belonged to a few rich families. They thought that the Church could lead people to the Kingdom of God while *at the same time* fighting for justice here on earth.

There were some in the country who thought that Romero would make a very good archbishop but not an outstanding one. Those who wanted the Church to change, to have more to do with the struggles of ordinary people for justice, were disappointed when Romero was chosen as Archbishop. They knew he was a good man but they did not think he would have anything to do with politics. On the other hand, the Government, the powerful military and those influential families who supported the unjust social system in El Salvador were happy to have Romero as Archbishop. They didn't expect him to interfere with the way the country was governed.

The choice of Romero as Archbishop of San Salvador was thus thought to be a means to heal the deep divisions within the country and within the Church. Only time would tell what sort of archbishop Romero was going to be. It was not long, though, before the Church and the people of El Salvador realized that he could not ignore injustice. But in El Salvador, to be a spokesperson for the poor was to oppose the Government, and to oppose the Government was to oppose the military and the rich families that influenced the politicians behind the scenes. By speaking for the poor, Romero made many enemies.

What Do You Think?

1. (a) Work in small groups and imagine that you need a new leader for your country. Make a list of the qualities you would expect a good leader to have. What would you say in a job description for your leader?

(b) Now imagine that you are a group of religious believers looking for a religious leader. What sort of person would be suitable for this position? If you were interviewing candidates on your shortlist for the post, what three questions would you ask them?

2. Oscar Romero wanted to be an ordinary priest. How may he have felt when he was asked to be a bishop, and then, only three years later, to become an archbishop? If you ask your headteacher to tell you what it felt like when they left the classroom to become the most senior teacher in the school, you may find this question easier to answer.

3. Many people thought that Romero would not be an outstanding archbishop. From what you have read about him so far, what do you think they meant? Think about why an archbishop might be described as 'outstanding'.

The Murder of Rutilio Grande

Many say that the turning-point for Romero came with the death of his friend the priest Rutilio Grande. It was 1977, the year of Romero's enthronement as Archbishop. Rutilio Grande spoke in a sermon about another priest, a friend of his who had been expelled from El Salvador for speaking up for the rights of the poor. It was a very powerful sermon.

In defence of his Christian friend and the Christian faith, Rutilio Grande said that it was a clear case of following the teachings of Jesus. A person could not claim to be a Christian in El Salvador if he or she simply ignored the violence against so many in the country. A person could not claim to be a Christian in El Salvador if he or she ignored the bombings, the illegal detentions, the torture, the callous murders of men, women and children.

Rutilio Grande also said that in El Salvador it was dangerous to be a Christian. To speak the Gospel message of God's love for the poor and suffering of this world was to risk persecution. This was a statement which the Government could not ignore.

Soon after, Rutilio Grande was murdered. He was driving by jeep with two companions, a 72-year-old man and a 16-year-old boy, on a routine journey through hilly countryside ripening with peasant crops. A loud burst of machine-gun fire came from the cover of the crops and all three travellers were killed. Many suspected the Government. Some of the bullets found on the road were the sort the military used. All three victims were buried, though, without a full investigation, the bullets still in their bodies.

Many saw these murders as a direct attack upon the Church itself. It was an assault which the Church could not ignore. Oscar Romero spent much time praying by the dead body of his friend. Perhaps it was in those prayerful moments of meditation on the violent end of one so dear to him that the Archbishop decided on his course of action.

What Do You Think?

1. Look at the things that Rutilio Grande said. What do you think he wanted Christians in El Salvador to do?

2. Why could the Church not ignore the murder of Rutilio Grande?

3. What sorts of feelings do you think Romero would have experienced being there beside the body of his murdered friend?

4. Romero prayed after the death of Rutilio Grande. Suggest some things he might have said to God.

Romero Speaks Out for the Oppressed

The Government probably hoped that the death of the Archbishop's friend, Rutilio Grande, would frighten the Church in El Salvador into silence. Far from discouraging the Church from getting involved in politics, the murder actually led Christians into direct confrontation with the Government. Over the next few years, it was increasingly common for the Church to be a target of violence. The Archbishop himself was threatened.

A government which is kept in power or is brought to power by military means is often known as a junta. In 1979, a military junta took power in El Salvador. Things seemed to be getting worse. The country was on the verge of civil war between the forces of the junta, with their rich supporters, and the poor of the country, who suffered great oppression. Kept poor by either the lack of work or low wages, the people were often powerless to protest for fear of violence from the military. The political situation was not helped by claims that aid money from abroad was being was used by the military. As Romero stated on one occasion, 'The aid is going directly to the security forces and it is well known that they are repressing the people.'

Who would speak for the ordinary people, those without education, those without power? It was Archbishop Oscar Romero who was the most powerful and influential voice of the Church and the spokesperson for the oppressed.

Just two days before his death, for example, Romero spoke of 'rampant terror' in the country of El Salvador. Most of the ordinary population was gripped by fear. The Government was making some reforms, giving land to the peasants. In those areas where there was no reform, however, Romero claimed: 'People are fleeing from the countryside, coming here to

San Salvador, or going into the mountains to sleep because if they are found by the security forces they will be killed. Armed troops search farmhouses, burn peasants' possessions and kill people. Terror is rampant in the countryside.'

Romero said that neither he nor the Church could stand idly by while such things happened. Neither he nor the Church could remain silent in the face of atrocities against the ordinary people of the country. The Archbishop stated clearly that the demands of the people were just but that if the people's anger at injustice spilled out into violence, then he could not support it.

Some of his critics, in both the Government and the Church, claimed that Romero was becoming too political. Romero replied that he was not following any particular political 'ideology'. As a leader of the Church he was simply following the teaching of the Gospels. Romero believed that the Gospels did not see a division between religion and everyday life. 'The Church cannot separate itself from the politics and the daily life of the people,' he said.

Many people listened to the sermons Romero preached openly in his cathedral in San Salvador. To the people of El Salvador at the time it must have seemed that Oscar Romero, the brave Archbishop, was a lone source of truth in a world of lies.

For many, what he said in his Sunday sermons inspired courage. Perhaps more important, in a world of fear and terror, Romero's preaching of the Gospel message of love and justice was a source of hope for the people.

His last sermon, on the Sunday before his death, was very significant. In it, Romero made a special request to those with belief in God and those of Christian faith within the security forces. He wanted these people within the security forces to renounce unjustified and unnecessary violence, the sort of excessively aggressive behaviour that the military had long used to suppress their own people. (See the extract from the sermon below left.)

It was a sermon which many believe cost him his life. A week after preaching these words Oscar Romero was assassinated.

What Do You Think?

1. Romero was clearly a brave person to speak out so openly when he knew that to do so was to risk his own life. What do you think gave him such courage?

2. Think about an occasion when you have had to be brave. If possible share some of your feelings about this experience with a friend.

3. When religious leaders speak about political issues they are often told, by politicians, to mind their own business and concentrate on teaching people about religious matters. How might a religious leader respond to this instruction?

Brothers, before obeying an order given to kill you ought to reflect on the law of God which says: do not kill. No soldier is obliged to obey an order that is contrary to the law of God. Nobody has to fulfil an immoral law. Now it is time that you recover your consciences and that you first obey your conscience rather than an order to sin. The Church, the defender of the rights of God, of the law of God, of the human dignity of the person, cannot remain silent before such an abomination. We want the Government to understand seriously that reforms are worth nothing if they are stained with so much blood. In the name of God, then, and in the name of those suffering, whose cries rise to the heavens, every day more clamouringly, I beg, I ask, I order you in the name of God: stop the repression.

From Oscar Romero's last sermon

The Funeral of the Archbishop

After the shooting of the Archbishop, violence erupted in the capital San Salvador. The newspapers reported that at least seventeen bombs had been exploded in the city. Word had got out about the assassination of the Archbishop and those political forces which opposed the Government were quick to blame them for the killing. The message soon spread: 'Romero is dead. The Government has killed the Archbishop.' The Government in its turn denied any involvement. Despite intensive investigations and many accusations, to this day no one has been prosecuted for the murder.

After the assassination, the armoured vehicles of the security forces patrolled the city in strength on the lookout for any disturbances. There were many troops in the streets around the Sacred Heart Basilica, the church where the body of Oscar Romero lay in state before it was moved to the cathedral for the funeral service. Before his funeral, thousands of people came to pay their last respects to this latest victim of political violence in El Salvador.

Visitors arrived from around the world to attend the funeral of Archbishop Romero. It was not only Church leaders who were there. Important politicians from many countries were also present. Romero had become a respected political as well as religious leader. Only the year before his murder, politicians from the United Kingdom had nominated him for the Nobel Peace Prize – it was the year when Mother Teresa actually won the prize. The funeral was bound to be a tense affair, especially given the history of violence in El Salvador.

In the days before the funeral crowds of people flooded into the city. The security forces patrolled everywhere. At the cathedral where Romero had so often preached, damage caused by bombs and bullets was

obvious. Inside, a group of monks, nuns and priests were gathered in a very public hunger strike. In protest at the killing of Romero, they were refusing to eat.

The day of the funeral was 30 March 1980. It was Palm Sunday, the day when Christians remember the triumphant procession of Jesus into Jerusalem before his death on the cross on Good Friday. All seemed calm enough but people were nervous. There were rumours that the funeral was going to be disrupted.

This Palm Sunday, as usual, there was a procession to the cathedral. As the procession moved slowly towards the cathedral square, the atmosphere was tense. As many as one hundred thousand people packed every available space outside the cathedral, waiting for the funeral service for the murdered Archbishop.

The solemn funeral service began in a dignified manner. During the sermon everyone listened intently to the words of remembrance for Oscar Romero, whose body lay in a glass-covered coffin.

One eyewitness was a European journalist, who described what happened.

Suddenly there was a huge explosion in the far, right-hand corner of the square. For a split second, there was the feeling of sitting in a theatre. What was happening in the square was too grotesque, too horrible to be reality. That corner of the square was ablaze and, as shots began to ring out, 100 000 people stampeded. Worst of all was the terrible crush. Some of the more agile clambered over the high, locked railings in front of the altar. But the children and many poor, overweight middle-aged women were being crushed against the bars.

In the square, people screamed and prayed as they ran clinging to their children. Inevitably families were separated in the panic, and the terror was magnified for those who had to continue on their own or double back for the elderly and the young. Glimpsing the early seconds of the tragedy, I was terrified ...

The coffin was taken inside ... The gates were opened and a huge mass of humanity tumbled through and clambered up the steps. Anyone who fell (and many did), would be trampled, some to death.

I was swept inside in the first tide of people, and took refuge behind a pillar. A young girl beside me was shivering with terror; she said that her elderly parents had been trampled down as they scrambled into the cathedral. She was sure they were dead. Outside more bombs were going off and shots were being fired ...

My young companion and I moved to a seat where we were ordered to put our hands over our heads and keep very low. Rumours that people in the cathedral had been shot in the head increased the panic. I was quite certain that I was going to die. Beside me an overweight pregnant woman in her late thirties went unconscious. Efforts were made to fan her back to life. They failed. The little girl had regained her composure but kept sobbing about her parents. All one could do was hold her hand tightly. Words of consolation and reassurance were quite superfluous. And as I looked at this little girl, old beyond her years, I was reminded that I might never see my own wife and children again.

(Dermot Keogh, *El Salvador's Martyr*. Dublin: Dominican Publications, 1981)

This disaster has come to be known as the 'Palm Sunday Massacre'.

After the horrific carnage at the funeral, different witnesses blamed differing sources for the panic and the deaths. The Government claimed that if armed opponents of their authority to rule had not appeared in the cathedral square then the violence that followed would not have occurred. A spokesperson for the junta claimed that it was all part of a plot to steal the body of the Archbishop and to provoke a full-scale civil war. This same spokesperson said that the security forces had not left their military barracks on the morning of the funeral.

Another witness, Monsignor O'Brien, claimed that there had been no attempt to snatch the corpse. Romero's body had been treated with great respect. He was also very certain that Salvadorian armed forces had opened fire on the crowd at the funeral from the second floor of the National Palace, which also stands in the cathedral square.

After the Palm Sunday Massacre, bodies lay in the cathedral awaiting identification. As people were arriving to identify the bodies, possibly of family members, two bombs were discovered in an upper floor of the cathedral.

To this day the argument over who was to blame for the massacre has never been really settled – just as no one has been successfully prosecuted for the murder of Archbishop Oscar Romero.

What Do You Think?

1. Why had visitors come from all over the world to attend the funeral of the Archbishop? What memories of El Salvador do you think they took home with them?

2. Oscar Romero was a candidate for the Nobel Peace Prize. If you were going to award a prize for promoting peace in today's world, who would be on your list of candidates? Suggest five people, well known or not so well known, and say why you have selected them.

3. From the account you have read, who do you think was responsible for the death of Archbishop Romero? Use evidence from this book to support your answer.

SHOTS AND PANIC AT ARCHBISHOP'S FUNERAL: 27 DIE

The blast from the M16 [assault rifle] mingled with the screams of the terrified mourners

Extracts from reports in *The Times* from a British journalist and MP both present at the funeral

...Women and children ... crushed to death in the stampede...

Guerillas carried pistols concealed under their T-shirts

Priest urged everyone to lie flat on the floor

A New Beginning for El Salvador?

In the years that followed the assassination of Archbishop Oscar Romero in March 1980, the violence in El Salvador escalated into a full-scale civil war. There were many terrible incidents in the war.

One of the most horrific events of the time occurred in December 1980. Four aid workers – three nuns and another woman – were raped and murdered in the most terrible of circumstances. People around the world were shocked at this sheer evil brutality. Another barbarous event took place in 1989 when six Jesuit priests, together with their cook and her daughter, were machine-gunned to death.

In all, it is estimated that the civil war in El Salvador cost the lives of 75 000 people. The Roman Catholic Church was often in the midst of the conflict.

In the early 1990s, though, with the help of the United Nations, a peace accord was signed by various factions. For the victims and families of victims of the civil war in El Salvador, on all sides of the conflict, it will take many years for the wounds of hatred and violence to be healed. A lasting peace is necessary if there is be justice for all, a cause for which Oscar Romero struggled and died.

In one of the last entries in his tape-recorded diary, Romero talks about a celebration of the Mass on the Catholic feast-day of St Joseph. This is what he says:

Wednesday, 19 March 1980. Today, St Joseph's feast, I celebrated the first Mass at the Colegio Cristobal Colon, run by the Josephite priests. I told them that St Joseph is the model for the man that our country needs today: with a commitment to a sense of justice, with a sense of collaboration and with a sense of faith.

During his life, Romero tried to put such ideals into practice. His religious belief was always a practical matter and his great desire was to see people work together for a better world. Romero shared, with all who would listen, a vision of justice in an unjust world.

Although no one has ever been punished for his murder, his life and martyrdom are remembered by millions. In a troubled world, Oscar Romero remains a sign of hope. Those who killed him may have thought that they would be silencing a powerful voice against injustice in El Salvador. They may have killed the man but his message of justice for all still lives even today.

What Do You Think?

1. The final paragraph of this story describes Oscar Romero as 'a sign of hope'. What do you think is meant by this?

Biographical
Notes

15 August 1917	Romero is born in Ciudad Barrios, El Salvador.
1930	**Starts at seminary in San Miguel.**
1937	Romero joins national seminary in the capital, San Salvador. A few months later he is sent to Rome to complete his theological studies.
4 April 1942	**Oscar Romero is ordained as priest.**
August 1943	Returns to El Salvador, having witnessed early years of Second World War in Europe.
From 1944	**Starts work as parish priest in Anamoros but after a few months is called by his bishop to work in San Miguel as the secretary of the diocese, a post which he holds for twenty-three years. Much of his pastoral work during this time centres on the cathedral parish.**
1962–65	Second Vatican Council held in Rome. By this time, Romero is one of the most important priests in the diocese, not only secretary to the bishop but in charge of the local seminary and editor of the diocesan newspaper.
September 1967	**Romero is appointed as Secretary-General of the National Bishops' Conference and moves to San Salvador.**
May 1968	Takes up an additional and important role for the Central American Bishops' Secretariat.
1968	**Council of Medellin held in Colombia.**
April 1970	Romero is made auxiliary (assistant) bishop in San Salvador. He becomes increasingly aware of the plight of the oppressed and the poor but resists the notion that the Church should be too involved in politics.
1974	**Romero is made Bishop of Santiago de Maria.**
1977	Romero is made Archbishop of San Salvador. His thinking on religion and politics develops. He sees an increasing need for the Church to have a voice in politics and becomes an outspoken critic of injustice and oppression.
24 March 1980	**Romero is assassinated.**
30 March 1980	'Palm Sunday Massacre'.

Things to Do

1 For display, draw a large map of Central America. Mark El Salvador and identify all the places where Oscar Romero grew up, studied, worked and died. Mark these places with symbols associated with what happened there, e.g. a bishop's mitre (hat).

2 Design a symbol suitable for a lapel badge supporting the bishops' stand against injustice in South America.

3 Imagine that it is 1968 and you are a European newspaper editor. Prepare a front page for your newspaper during the bishops' conference at Medellin. Include a headline and a brief account of why the conference is being held in South America. What other stories might you decide to put on the front page, local, national or international? Remember that the year is 1968. Also include an advertisement which might (indirectly) contrast living standards in Europe and South America.

4 Find out about links between local churches and communities in poorer parts of the world. Do they support aid agencies such as CAFOD or Christian Aid? Find out what sort of development work is being done at present by these agencies, in South America and El Salvador in particular. Make a display or write up your findings for a school newspaper.

5 Make a collage to illustrate issues of social injustice in the world. You might choose to focus upon the contrasts between rich and poor which still divide the world.

6 Script, role-play and, if possible, film on video an imaginary television interview with Romero on the evening before he preaches his final sermon. The producer has told the interviewer to find out as much as possible about the life and work of this outspoken archbishop. What questions are asked and how does Romero respond? Alternatively, script, role-play and record the imaginary interview as a radio programme.

7 If Romero had won the Nobel Peace Prize, he would have been expected to make an acceptance speech thanking the committee for awarding him the prize and highlighting some issues connected with his work. Imagine that Romero did win the prize. What do you think he might have said in his acceptance speech? Make notes then present your speech.

8 The year before Oscar Romero's murder, politicians from the United Kingdom nominated him for the Nobel Peace Prize. Another nominee was Mother Teresa.

(a) Research the life and work of Mother Teresa. (See *In the Streets of Calcutta* in this series.)

(b) Divide into two groups and write a speech in support of one of these two candidates.

(c) Hold a debate and vote to decide whether your class would have given the prize to Oscar Romero or to Mother Teresa.

9 Sometimes people organize public events such as concerts with the aim of raising the profile of human rights. Artists are encouraged to perform without charge.

(a) In groups, imagine you are running such a concert and talk about how you could persuade famous stars to take part. Draft a letter inviting a star to perform at the event. The letter should explain the nature and purpose of the concert and highlight two human rights issues.

(b) Imagine that you are a famous star and you have agreed to perform the opening number at such a concert. Write your own song or poem concerning any issue of injustice in the world today.

Questions for Assessment or Examination Candidates

10 In his diary entry for the Sunday before his death, Archbishop Romero referred to his last sermon in the cathedral:

Sunday, 16 March 1980. Today I highlighted the repression, which has not ended but, instead, is getting worse. It is causing great pain and the Church must denounce it.

In Luke 4:18, Jesus reads in the synagogue from the words of the Jewish prophet Isaiah:

He has sent me to bring good news to the poor, to proclaim liberty to captives and to set the downtrodden free.

This verse in the Gospel of Luke shows just how 'revolutionary' is the Gospel message. It is a teaching about serving others which many faiths might share. Oscar Romero organized and lived his life around this principle of faith in action. Give examples from the scriptures of a faith you have studied of other teachings about serving others or helping the poor and oppressed.

11 Answer **one** of the following structured essays:

(a) Why do you think a command against murder is a common feature of the world's religions? (5 marks)

(b) In what ways did Oscar Romero fight for basic human rights? (5 marks)

(c) 'Bishops should keep out of politics and concentrate on the spiritual and moral development of church members.' Do you agree? Give your reasons, showing that you have thought about more than one point of view. (10 marks)

OR

(a) Explain the teachings of one religious founder about how the poor should be treated. (5 marks)

(b) Outline the problems faced by poor people in a country where resources are not fairly divided. (10 marks)

(c) 'It is the duty of all religious believers to work to ease the plight of the poor.' Do you agree? Give your reasons, showing that you have thought about more than one point of view. (5 marks)

Religious and Moral Education Press
An imprint of Chansitor Publications Ltd,
a wholly owned subsidiary of
Hymns Ancient & Modern Ltd
St Mary's Works, St Mary's Plain
Norwich, Norfolk NR3 3BH

First published 1998

ISBN 1 85175 147 5

Designed and typeset by
TOPICS – The Creative Partnership,
Exeter

Illustrations by Brian Platt

Printed in Great Britain by
Brightsea Press, Exeter for
Chansitor Publications Ltd, Norwich

Notes for Teachers

The first Faith in Action books were published in the late 1970s and the series has remained popular with both teachers and pupils. However, much in education has changed over the last twenty years, such as the development of both new examination syllabuses in Religious Studies and local agreed syllabuses for Religious Education which place more emphasis on pupils' own understanding, interpretation and evaluation of religious belief and practice, rather than a simple knowledge of events. This has encouraged us to amend the style of the Faith in Action Series to make it more suitable for today's classroom.

The aim is, as before, to tell the stories of people who have lived and acted according to their faith, but we have included alongside the main story questions which will encourage pupils to think about the reasons for the behaviour of our main characters and to empathize with the situations in which they found themselves. We hope that pupils will also be able to relate some of the issues in the stories to other issues in modern society, either in their own area or on a global scale.

The 'What Do You Think?' questions may be used for group or class discussion or for short written exercises. The 'Things to Do' at the end of the story include ideas for longer activities and more-structured questions suitable for assessment or examination practice.

In line with current syllabus requirements, as Britain is a multifaith society, Faith in Action characters will be selected from a wide variety of faith backgrounds and many of the questions may be answered from the perspective of more than one faith.

CMB, 1997

Acknowledgements
Cover photograph reproduced by kind permission of Carlos Reyes-Manzo/Andes Press Ager